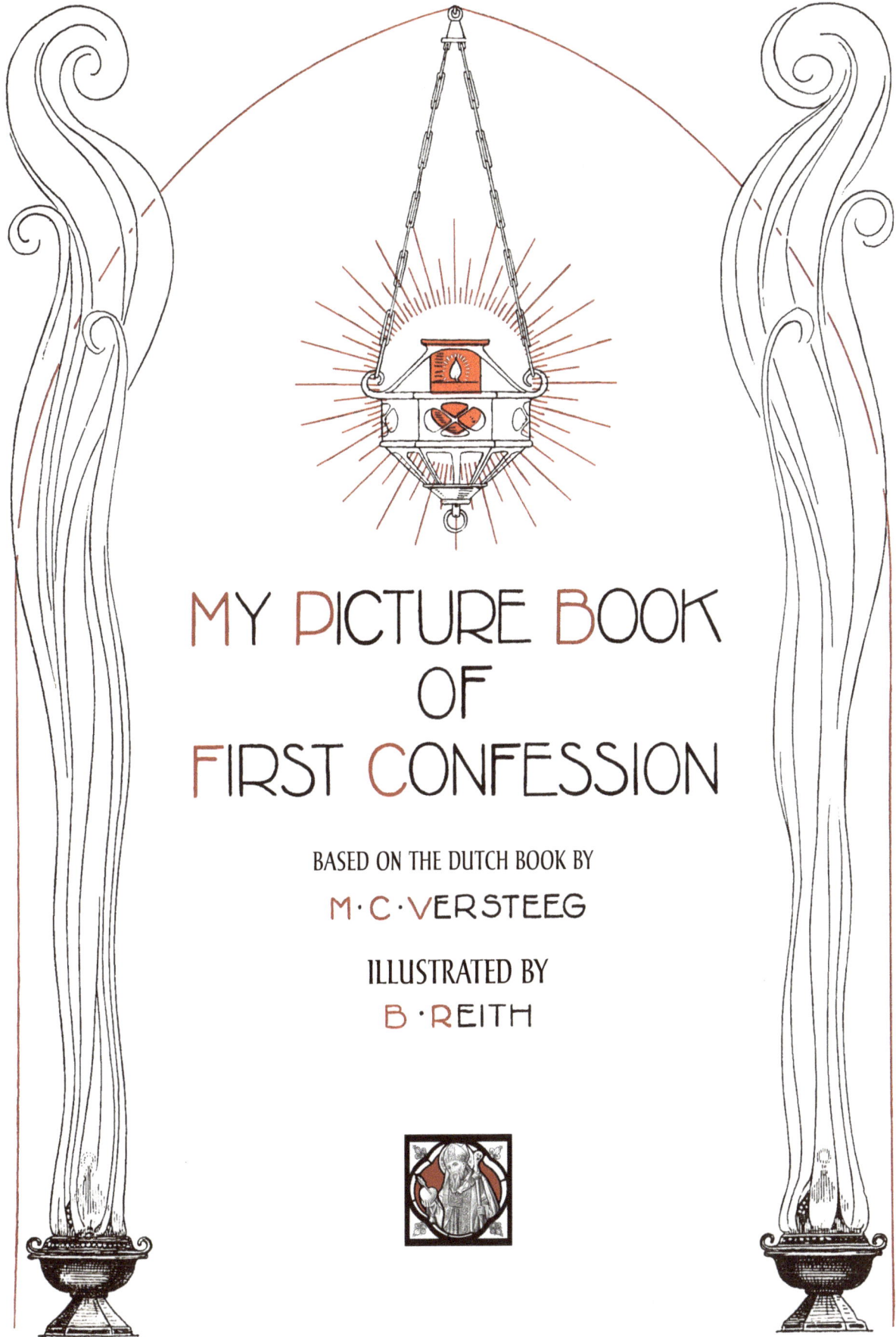

MY PICTURE BOOK
OF
FIRST CONFESSION

BASED ON THE DUTCH BOOK BY

M·C·VERSTEEG

ILLUSTRATED BY

B·REITH

· ST. AUGUSTINE ACADEMY PRESS · HOMER GLEN ·

·REITH·

A child is born, and his parents are so happy! They treasure every one of his tiny, precious fingers and toes, and his soft, sleepy little cheeks. He is so sweet and helpless, and needs the love and care of his parents as he grows.

Little baby Joseph also needs the love and care of God and His angels to help him grow as a good child who will go to heaven someday. So his parents bring him to church as soon as possible so that he can become a child of God through Baptism.

When God first gives us life, He gives us a *soul*. The soul is the part of us that thinks and learns, and chooses between good and bad. Even after our body dies, our soul will go on living forever. But when we are first born, our beautiful soul has a very sad stain.

This stain is not our fault. Long, long ago in the Garden of Eden, our first parents, Adam and Eve, chose to disobey God. By this choice they lost the gift of God's *grace* and stained their souls with sin. They had no way to remove this stain, and souls that are stained cannot enter heaven. And this stain passed on to their children, and to all children born since that time. We call this stain *Original Sin*.

But God had a plan to remove that stain. He sent His beloved Son, Jesus, to live among us and teach us, and even give up His life for us on the cross. He restored to us the gift of *grace* that would remove our stain of original sin and allow us to enter heaven.

How do we apply this grace to our souls and remove the stain? *Through the Sacrament of Baptism.* This is why little Joseph's parents have brought him to Church today. Here they are at the Baptismal font, which is filled with Holy Water. Here the Holy Ghost will wash away the stain of Original Sin from Joseph's soul. How do we know this? We cannot see a soul! And we cannot see the Holy Ghost. But we do know that water washes our bodies. So in the Sacrament of Baptism, God uses Holy Water as a *sign that we can see*, to wash away our Original Sin.

Before we can be baptized, we must choose to belong to God, and promise to take good care of our souls. Can a little baby choose, or promise? Of course not. But Joseph's mother and father know that his soul will be safest in God's hands—it would not do to wait! Only a nice, clean soul will be pleasing in God's sight. So until little Joseph is old enough to choose and to promise, there is someone who will make the choice and the promise for him. This is his Godfather and Godmother.

Once these solemn promises are made, the priest pours holy water over Joseph's head and says "I baptize thee in the name of the Father, and of the Son, and of the Holy Ghost." See how heaven opens up with great joy as God and His Angels smile down upon this pure, gleaming white soul that has now been washed clean. How God our Father loves His new little child!

The Pastor will write Joseph's name in the great record book of the parish. But more importantly, the angels have written Joseph's name in the great Book of Life. He is now a true Child of God and heir of heaven.

When little Joseph was baptized, the priest gave him a white robe as a *sign we can see* of his fresh clean soul. And he said to mother and father and Joseph's godparents, "Receive this white garment and see thou carry it unstained." Mother and Father take this promise very seriously. They will help Joseph to carry unstained his garment of *grace*. They will help him to keep his soul pure and clean.

Joseph's Guardian Angel is there to help too. Oh yes, Joseph has his very own Angel! Our souls are so precious to God, that He gives each of us an Angel to guard and guide us, and bring us to heaven one day. Why? Because He sent His only Son, Jesus, to die on the cross for us, that our souls might be cleaned and come to heaven. Oh, what a price He paid for our souls! It would grieve Him to lose even one. So he places each of us in the care of one of His angels. That is how much God loves us.

Because the Angels love God, they love to serve Him. And they love what He loves. How our Guardian Angels love us! They never rest night or day, but watch over us always. Who knows how many dangers our good Angels have protected us from? With love and care, Joseph's angel wraps his wings around him as he sleeps. He looks down upon Joseph's beautiful pure soul, and is so glad to be its protector.

Our Guardian Angels see more than we can see. Joseph's angel is pointing up to heaven. What does he see there? Oh look! Around God's mighty throne there are many smaller golden thrones. How beautiful they are! And one of them has Joseph's name upon it. God has prepared it especially for him. No one else may take it. Joseph has only to be good and keep his soul free from the sins that will stain it, and that throne may be his—forever!

All the angels and saints in heaven look forward to the day when they may welcome Joseph into heaven. Until then, Mother and Father will be sure to ask for their help in guiding little Joseph on the surest path. Those in heaven love God very much and want us to be happy with Him forever. So they will be glad to pray for Joseph.

Joseph is now growing bigger. He can sit up and crawl and play with his toys. His soul is still so innocent and pure.

When he is old enough to talk, mother will teach Joseph to pray. She knows it is important always to pray. We like to talk to our friends and loved ones. God is our very best friend. He loves us more than anyone else does, even more than our mother and father do. So of course, we must not forget to talk to Him. We must remember to tell Him we love Him, and ask Him for the things we need. He is always happy to give us what we need. But He likes to be asked first.

God in heaven hears little Joseph's prayers, and gives him many blessings.

Joseph is still too small to know the difference between good and evil. Sometimes his mother has to say, "No Joseph! That is naughty!" She must help him learn to be honest, truthful, patient and kind to others. She remembers the promises made at Baptism and she wants to help him keep his white robe of grace clean and pure.

God looks down from heaven, always hoping to see that Joseph is obeying his father and mother. God loves those who are obedient. Why? Because His laws protect us from harm, and from staining our white garment with sin. Oh, how happy we all would be if we always obeyed God's laws! If everyone were always honest, truthful, patient and kind, there would be no sadness and we would all go to heaven.

But it is not easy to be good all the time. Joseph knows he must wait until after dinner before he may eat a cookie. But they smell so good, and they look good too. And he is hungry. Oh, and there is the devil! He tells Joseph, "Go ahead! Eat the cookie!"

Oh dear! Will Joseph run away from this temptation? No. He takes the cookie. Oh, how sad God is! For now Joseph has disobeyed and stolen a cookie. He has committed a small sin—a *venial sin*—and made his soul dirty with a little stain. No longer is his soul beautiful and pure as it was before.

When Mother asks Joseph, "Did you take a cookie?" does he tell the truth? Oh no! He says little sister did it. He has told a lie. Oh, how unhappy his Guardian Angel looks! If only Joseph had told the truth and said he was sorry, Mother and God might have forgiven him. Instead, now there is another spot on Joseph's soul.

If Joseph continues to sin in this way, his soul will become dirtier and dirtier. This will make it harder to hear the warning voice of his good angel, and make it easier for the devil to tempt him to commit bigger and bigger sins. That is how the thief in the third picture became a bad man. He was not afraid of little sins...so they got bigger.

Big sins, like stealing lots of money, make our whole soul black and ugly, and our white garment of grace is lost completely. A soul like that cannot come to heaven and be close to God. Sins like this are called *Mortal Sins* because they kill the life of God's grace in us.

But there is still hope for that naughty thief. Remember, God wants us all to come to heaven. So he has made a way for both Joseph and the naughty thief to clean the spots from their soul, restore the garment of grace and make it beautiful again. He does this through the *Sacrament of Penance*.

In the Sacrament of Penance, we must confess our sins to a priest. The priest takes the place of Our Lord himself, for God has promised to forgive what the priest forgives. Here, in the Confessional, the priest does just what Our Lord would do: He listens patiently to those who come to confess their sins. He asks them if they are truly sorry. Then He takes away the spots from their souls, and says to them, just as Jesus once said, "Thy sins are forgiven thee—go now, and sin no more." Oh, what a good and loving God we have, who always forgives us when we tell him we are sorry!

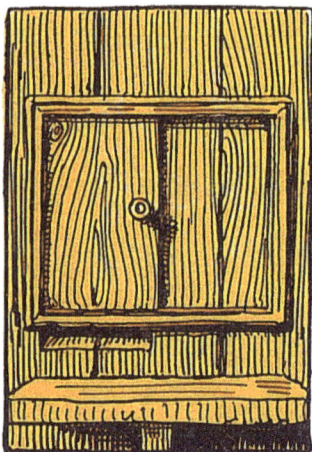

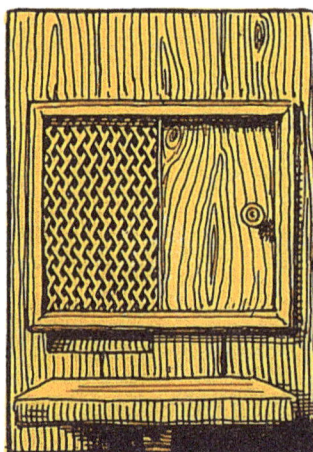

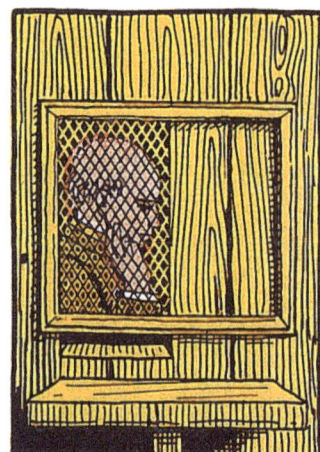

oseph and Susan are going to confession today. They must faithfully tell the priest all the naughty things they have done, so that all the spots may be removed from their souls. Is it easy to remember all our sins, or to see those spots on our souls? No, we cannot see those spots like our Good Angel can, and we forget our sins so easily. But James and Susan know just who to ask for help!

First they will ask Mother Mary. She loves us and cares for our souls. She wants all of us to be dear brothers and sisters of her beloved Son. She is always quick to help us when we pray to her. So they ask Our Lady, "Please help me to make a good confession." Then they say the *Hail Mary* three times.

Next, they will ask one who sees and knows all, who is a faithful guide to our souls: The Holy Ghost. He will shine a light into their souls and lend them the knowledge to see their faults more clearly.

COME HOLY GHOST

They say, "Come, Holy Ghost, from heaven on high. Help me to know my sins, and to confess them well. Good Holy Ghost, help me also to be truly sorry for my sins, and to sin no more."

Now they are going to quietly think. Look how they cover their eyes so that they will not be distracted. Mary helps, and so does the Holy Ghost. With this help, they will surely find their sins! They will find them as they think carefully of the things they have done in church, at home, in school, and around town.

Let us look at each of these places with them, and see where their sins may be found.

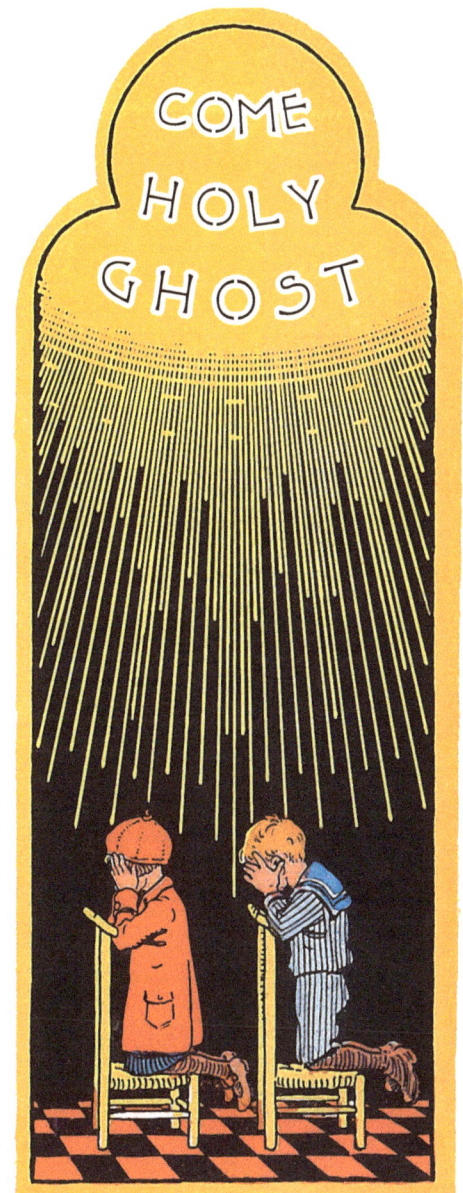

Because our first duty is to God and His Church, we will look here first.

We know that the Third Commandment tells us to keep holy the Lord's Day. We also know that God's laws keep us from harm and help make us fit for heaven. So of course we want to follow His Commandments. We keep the Third Commandment by going to Mass on Sunday, and by resting from work.

Have I missed Mass on Sunday, or did I play or do something else instead? Or was I late for Mass through my own fault, because I would not get ready in time? Did I do work on Sunday that could have been done another day?

If the answer to these questions is yes, I must confess this, for I have sinned.

When Jesus was a child, He gave us an example of attention and reverence when He prayed in the temple. At Mass, the priest recreates Christ's sacrifice on the cross for us. Jesus is truly present there with us, in the bread and wine that become His Body and Blood. This is the most holy moment of all. We should not give our attention to other things when Jesus Himself has come from high heaven to be with us.

If my mind wanders at Mass, do I try to bring my attention back to Jesus? During the very solemn parts of Mass, do I keep my eyes on the altar, or am I looking around at my friends or other distractions?

If I have not tried hard to pay attention during Mass, I must confess this.

The very best way to give our gift of love to God at Mass is to follow along with the prayers of the Mass, and to offer up our own sacrifices along with the priest as he offers up Jesus' sacrifice for us. But there are many other ways for us to show God our Love. He will be pleased if we give Him our hearts, and do our best to pray and to think of Him.

Do I try always during Mass to think of God, to talk to Him, and to thank Him for His many gifts? Do I refrain from talking, laughing or playing? Do I leave my toys, games and other such things at home, where they belong?

If I have not done my best to give my heart to God during Mass, but have talked or played instead, then I must confess this.

Now let us look for sins that we may have committed at home.

Every day the Child Jesus faithfully prayed to His Father in Heaven. All that he would do or say that day, He offered to God. We can make everything we do each day a little gift to God if we follow the example of the Child Jesus. We ought to pray in the morning when we wake, at mealtimes, and at night before we go to bed.

When we forget to pray each day, we do not invite God into our lives. If our only thoughts are of pleasing ourselves with our food, our toys and other amusements, we will think less and less of our Father in heaven, and this will cause us to get further away from Him and from the happiness that awaits us in heaven.

Have I forgotten to say my morning and night prayers? Have I said them in a hurry, or without paying attention to what I am saying? Have I neglected to pray before and after meals?

If I have not prayed as I should, I will confess this.

The Child Jesus was always obedient to Mary and Joseph, and helped them with their work. Just think! He was God, but he became a little boy and worked in the kitchen, and the yard, and the workshop. All so that I might learn that obedience and hard work are the way to heaven! I must follow His example, and obey my parents in all things.

When my parents ask me to do something, do I do it promptly, and without complaining? Or do I care more about what I want to do, and grumble and avoid doing what I have been asked?

If I have been disobedient to my parents, if I have refused to do what they ask, or if I have been lazy in doing it, I must confess this.

God has entrusted us to our Mother and Father, and they must work hard to clothe and feed and care for us. They must also teach us God's laws so that we may be fit for heaven one day. When they ask us to be good, and patient, and kind, and not fight with our brothers and sisters, it is our duty to honor and obey them. We must not be unruly or spiteful, and we must never be disrespectful toward them.

Do I ignore my parents' warnings, or treat them with disrespect? Do I talk back to them? When they punish me for being disobedient, do I accept my punishment as I ought, or do I lash out or sulk?

If I have been disrespectful to my parents, I must confess this.

Let us look for other sins that may be committed in the home.

We must not steal. When we take things that do not belong to us, we are hurting others. Remember that Jesus has said, "as long as you did it to one of these my least brethren, you did it to Me." When I hurt others, I hurt Jesus.

Joseph is alone in the room, and the bowl of apples looks so delicious! "No one is here," says the voice of the devil, "no one will know if you take just one!" But Joseph does not want to disobey and make Our Lord sad. He leaves the room to get away from the temptation.

What does Angela do when the devil tempts her? She does not run away when the devil whispers in her ear. She takes the apple and hides and eats it. But in her heart, as she eats the apple, Angela knows she has done wrong. And God sees it too.

Have I been honest, and fled from the temptations of the devil? Or have I given in and taken what did not belong to me? If I have stolen anything, even something little, I must confess this.

We must be truthful. It may seem like a little thing to bend the truth in order to get out of trouble, but lying is like a dangerous disease, because it quickly becomes a habit, and makes us ugly in the sight of heaven. And think how the devil uses lies to trick us. We never want to be like him. So we must be brave and do what is right.

Susan has broken a teacup. She is afraid of being punished, but she knows that God loves those who are truthful. So she bravely tells the truth when Mother asks what happened. Mother is proud of Susan for telling the truth and together they clean up the pieces.

Nathan was playing with his father's pipe and dropped and broke it. Father asks how this happened. Nathan knows that father has told him many times not to play with his pipe, so he decides to blame it on his baby brother. Oh, how sad his guardian angel is!

Have I told lies? If I have been untruthful, even in small things, I must confess this.

Jesus became a little Child to be our example in all things. *He always played fairly and nicely* with his friends. When we follow His example, we will be happy when we play. How it pleases God to see children merrily laughing and playing together as in the picture on the left! They are all being kind to one another.

But the children on the right are quarrelsome. They yell, say mean things, cheat at games, and hit, kick and scratch each other. They are not happy. Their selfishness and anger cast many spots all over their souls and make Our Lord very sad.

Have I played unfairly, or been quarrelsome? Have I used bad language, or hurt others out of selfishness or anger? Have I refused to be kind to my brothers and sisters because I was in a bad temper? If I have done any of these things, I must confess this.

Now let us look to see if we have committed any sins at school.

Good children like to go to school. They know this is what their parents want for them, and that it is for their own good. Learning their lessons and completing their schoolwork every day helps them to grow up to be steady and responsible, so that someday they too will be good fathers and mothers, or maybe even priests or religious.

Children who do not want to go to school, who do not complete their lessons, or sneak away to play or be idle, form habits of willfulness and laziness instead. They disobey God and they disobey their parents. This is not the path to heaven.

If I have missed classes, either through carelessness or willfulness, or if I have been lazy and failed to do my lessons as I ought, then I must confess this.

Children go to school to learn. Even if our lessons are hard, or the subject is not our favorite, we must try our best, be quiet and still, pay attention, and keep order in the classroom. By being respectful, we make it easier for all to learn and grow in virtue.

Misbehaving in class may seem like fun, but it harms the other children by disrupting their opportunity to learn. It also makes Our Lord sad, because it does not show the respect that is due to our teachers, who stand in the place of our parents in the classroom. And if we set a bad example for others, and they too disobey and are disrespectful, then we are partially to blame for their sin, and we share the spots on our soul. Oh, how sad this is in God's sight!

If I have been disrespectful to my teachers in my words or actions, If I have failed to pay attention in the classroom, or if I have been deliberately disruptive during class time, I must confess this.

We must be diligent. When Adam and Eve had to leave Paradise because of their sin, God told them they must work. Our fathers and mothers must work too, so that we may have food, clothes and a tidy home. When I am not home to help them, my work is to learn at school. By doing this work well, I will gain the good habits I need to work well and obey God when I am older.

When we are idle, it is far easier for the devil to settle down next to us and whisper in our ear. If we give him such an easy time, oh, how many things he may trick us into doing! No, it is far safer to keep busy and avoid his temptations.

If I have avoided schoolwork or other duties, or if I have been idle when I should have been diligent, I must confess this.

If you tell your father you have ruined your new shoes, but you don't apologize for doing it, do you think that he will easily forgive you? Or will he be disappointed? If it is hard for your father to forgive you without saying you are sorry, how can we expect God to forgive our sins, if we are not sorry for them?

And how will God know that we are sincerely sorry? In the very same way as your own father. If you tell him you are sorry for ruining your new shoes, he will know you are sincerely sorry if you *promise not to do it again*, and you *try hard to keep that promise*.

This is what Our Lord asks of us in Confession. Only that we tell the priest our sins, and be truly sorry for them, by promising to be better. Oh, how generous God is, to make it so easy to be forgiven!

The first thing we ought to do, then, in order to make sure that we have contrition for our sins, is to pray for God's help to be sorry.

> Dear Lord, I am going to confess my sins now. I want to be forgiven so that I can be good friends with You and go to heaven someday. Please help me to be truly sorry for my sins and not to do them again. Our Father...
> O Mary, dear Mother in Heaven, pray for me to your Son, so that I may have true regret for my sins and be brave in resisting them. Hail Mary...
> Dear Guardian Angel, you are always at my side to guide me toward heaven. Help me now to put my feet on the right path by confessing my sins with true contrition. Help me never to sin again.

There are many things we can think about that will help us to have sorrow for our sins. Here we see that Susan is looking up to the sky, and imagining how wonderful heaven must be. It makes her sad to think that her sins may keep her from being able to go there. She feels contrition for her sins because they cause her to lose heaven.

Joseph knows that his sins deserve punishment, and he thinks of the poor souls in purgatory. They died with the ugly spots of sin on their souls, and now they suffer while they wait for those spots to be removed, so that they may be with God. He thinks of the fire that must burn those spots off, and he is afraid. He feels contrition for his sins because he does not want to suffer in purgatory.

The man has a mortal sin on his soul, and he knows that this separates him from God completely. How terrible are his thoughts as he imagines the fires of hell! The souls who suffer in purgatory know that someday they will finally see the face of God smiling upon them. But there is a great chasm surrounding hell that cannot be crossed. Those who go there have been careless of their friendship with God and have chosen to do what is wrong. Now they must take the consequences of their choice—forever! The man shudders with terror at this horrible thought. He feels contrition for his sins because he fears the pains of hell.

All of these ways of having contrition are enough for God to forgive our sins in the Sacrament of Penance. But the best kind of contrition is to be sorry for our sins not only for our own sake, but *for God's sake*, because He is so good and we do not want to make Him sad. To get this kind of contrition, let us walk the way of the Cross with Jesus, and see what He suffered for the sake of your sins and mine.

Dear Jesus has been bound to a pillar. Jesus, our God, who healed the sick and cured the lepers, is being punished like a criminal. See how the soldiers scourge him with their whips! Feel the sting as each cruel stroke lands upon his poor back. Oh! Jesus, my God and my Creator, you are bleeding from all these blows!

Dear child, each of these painful lashes I suffer for the sins of men, who let anger and hatred rule them instead of patience and forgiveness. When they hurt one another, they are really hurting Me. If you would comfort Me, please remember Me, and sin no more.

Dearest Jesus, I am sad to think that when I am angry and mean to others, it is as if I myself had scourged You. You suffered to take away my sins. Help me to remember You. Help me to be patient and forgiving, and never to hurt you again. Help me to be good, dear Jesus. I love You.

Now the cruel soldiers have placed a crown of thorns on Jesus' head and are pushing it down with their sticks. Look how the sharp points pierce his skin and spoil His beautiful face! Oh, and now they are mocking him and spitting on Him. Jesus, my God and my King, deserving all our love and worship, how can you bear these insults?

My dear child, I suffer for the sins of men, who selfishly forget God, and do only as they please. When they put themselves first, they put Me last, and they make a mockery of Me. If you would comfort Me, please remember Me, and sin no more.

Dearest Jesus, I am ashamed to think that when I am selfish and careless, it is as if I myself had mocked You and spit upon You. You suffered to take away my sins. Help me to remember You. Help me to serve others instead of myself, and never to hurt you again. Help me to be good, dear Jesus. I love You.

The soldiers have laid the heavy cross on Jesus' back and now they force Him to carry it through the streets. Look how it presses against His cruel crown of thorns, and all the many sores on His poor back! Jesus, my God and my Savior, You are so tired, and the cross so heavy, that You fall three times.

My dear child, this heavy cross I carry represents the weight of all the sins of the world—all that came before Me, and all that are yet to come. Each time you sin, you add to its weight. If you would comfort Me, please remember Me, and sin no more.

Dearest Jesus, I am sorry to think that each time I disobey God's laws, I am making your heavy cross even heavier. You suffered to take away my sins. Help me to remember You. Help me to be obedient, and never to hurt you again. Help me to be good, dear Jesus. I love You.

The soldiers have nailed Jesus' hands and feet to the cross. Look how the blood from all his wounds stains the ground! The pain is too much to bear, and now He is dying for us. Oh Jesus, my God and my all, you did all this for me!

My dear child, I willingly chose to suffer all this pain, and even death, so that you would know that nothing is too much for my love to bear for your sake. See now how much I want you to be happy in heaven forever with me. If you would comfort Me, please remember Me, and sin no more.

Dearest Jesus, the precious blood you have shed opened the gates of heaven—it gave me the grace of baptism—it restores my soul in Confession—it will strengthen me against sin when I receive it in the Eucharist. You suffered to take away my sins. Help me to remember You. Help me to be willing to suffer for your sake, and never to hurt you again. Help me to be good, dear Jesus. I love You.

ow that Joseph and Susan have completed the necessary preparation, they are ready to go to confession. Let us see what happens. Many confessionals look like this one (they usually have curtains or doors, but we are going to see inside for now). The priest sits in the center, and has a little door on each side. Susan is ready to confess, so he has opened the little door on that side so that he may hear her confession. The door on the other side is closed. Joseph cannot hear.

As soon as the door opens, Susan says, "Bless me, Father, for I have sinned." And of course, the priest gladly gives his blessing, just as Our Lord would. He wants Susan to have a good confession.

Next, it is good to tell the priest how long it has been since your last confession. Susan says, "It has been one month since my last confession." If this is your first confession, you may simply tell the priest that.

Now Susan must tell the priest all her sins. She knows that the priest will listen patiently, just as Jesus himself would, so she is not afraid or nervous. If she forgets something, or has a question, she knows she can ask and he will help her.

It helps her remember her sins when she thinks about the ones she has committed in Church, at home, at school, and around town. She also tells the priest how many times (or about how many times) she has committed each sin. When she has finished telling all her sins, she says: "For these sins, and all the sins of my past life, I am truly sorry, especially for the sin of _____." You should do the same, and pick the sin you know you are sorriest for.

Now it is the priest's turn. He may give her some good advice about how to do better, but most importantly, he will give Susan a *penance*. Her sins deserve to be punished by God, but as we know, Jesus paid for all our sins already. So instead, she must perform some good work, called a penance, in order to help make amends for her sins. It is usually something small—perhaps three Hail Marys, or some other prayers.

Susan knows it is very important to listen attentively to what the priest tells her. There is no need to think back over her sins to see if she has forgotten any. As long as she is truly sorry, all of them will be forgiven, even if she has accidentally forgotten one.

If she didn't hear correctly, or doesn't understand what penance she is to do, she will politely ask the priest to repeat or explain. She wants to be sure she does what he asks.

When this is finished, the priest then asks Susan to recite the *Act of Contrition*.

While she does this, the priest prays softly for her. Then he makes the Sign of the Cross and says, "I absolve thee from thy sins, In the Name of the Father, and of the Son, and of the Holy Ghost." While he says this, Susan also makes the sign of the cross, and together with the priest, says, "Amen."

When the priest says these words, God himself now washes away the spots from Susan's soul, and gives her many graces to help her to be brave and avoid sin in the future. Oh, this is the best part of confession! God is pleased to see Susan's soul so beautiful and clean again, and so is her Guardian Angel. But most of all, Susan is happy in knowing that God has forgiven her and she is keeping her soul ready for heaven.

Now they are finished, and the priest says to Susan, "Go in peace, your sins are forgiven." She thanks him and leaves the confessional.

But all is not over yet. Not quite. When Susan has left the confessional, she goes quietly to her place and kneels down and says her penance right away, so that she does not forget. And now her confession is done.

Before she goes home, however, she remembers that she had asked for help to make a good confession, and all good children know that it is polite to say "thank you" when someone has done something for us. Susan will not forget to thank God, and Our Lady and the Holy Ghost, who have helped her.

She says:
Dear Lord, thank you for giving me the grace to confess my sins well.
I thank you with the good thief, and St. Peter, and St. Mary Magdalene, and all the saints in heaven whose sins you forgave.
I thank you with my good Angel, who is so glad to see my soul clean and ready for heaven again.
Help me, Lord, to keep my good resolutions, and not to give up trying if I break them sometimes.
Our Father…

Then she thanks Our Lady:
O Mother Mary, thank you for helping me to confess my sins well.
Please pray for me, that I may not sin again and hurt your dear son Jesus.
Hail Mary…

And then she thanks the Holy Ghost:
O Holy Ghost, thank you for helping me to know my sins and confess them well.
Help me to keep my soul clean.
Glory Be…

And now Susan is finished and she can go home happy.

Order for Confession

BEFORE CONFESSION:

1. I must pray for the grace to make a good confession.

O Mary, please help me to make a good confession...(3 Hail Marys)

Come, Holy Ghost, from heaven on high. Help me to know my sins, to confess them well, to be truly sorry, and to sin no more.

2. I must carefully examine my conscience.

Church:
Have I attended Mass on all Sundays and Holy Days?...
Am I on time?...
Have I been respectful in Church?...

Home:
Am I obedient and respectful to my parents?...
Have I stolen things at home or from neighbors?...
Have I told the truth at home?...
Have I played nicely with my brothers and sisters or neighbors?...

School:
Am I obedient at school?...
Have I stolen anything at school?...
Have I told the truth at school?...
Have I played nicely at school?...
Have I been destructive of things belonging to others or to the school?...

On the Town:
Have I been respectful of others?...
Have I stolen anything?...
Have I been destructive or careless of other people's property?...

3. I must take time and care to have contrition for my sins.

IN THE CONFESSIONAL:

1. Blessing: "Bless me, Father, for I have sinned..."

2. Tell your sins...

3. Penance: be sure to ask the priest to repeat or explain if you didn't understand.

4. Say the Act of Contrition.

AFTER CONFESSION:

1. Pray your Penance.

2. Give thanks:

Dear Lord, thank you for giving me the grace to confess my sins well...*Our Father...*

O Mother Mary, thank you for helping me...*Hail Mary...*

O Holy Ghost, thank you for helping me to know my sins...*Glory Be...*

Here are four people in line for confession. Let us see what each one does.

1. The first is a man. He examines his conscience and finds two mortal sins and five venial sins.

What should he confess?

The Catechism tells us that all of our mortal sins must be confessed. It is good to confess our venial sins too, but we must not neglect to confess the mortal sins for any reason.

Of course, the man wants to make a good confession and he wants to confess all of his sins.

When he enters the confessional, he tells the priest all his sins, beginning with the first mortal sin, and then the second mortal sin, and then all the little venial sins.

Did that man have a good confession? Yes, he confessed all his sins, he was truly sorry for them, and he has resolved to avoid them in future. All of his sins are now absolved and cleaned off of his soul, and it is clean and pure and fit for heaven again. He leaves the confessional happy.

BEFORE CONFESSION

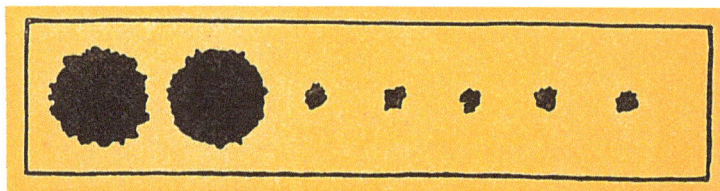

AFTER CONFESSION

2. The next is a woman. She has examined her conscience and has found 3 mortal sins and six venial sins.

What should she confess?

She may confess the venial sins if she chooses. This is a good practice. But she must confess all three of her mortal sins.

But the woman is ashamed of one of those mortal sins. So ashamed that she feels she cannot tell it to anyone—not even to the priest.

She goes into the confessional and she confesses the first mortal sin, and the second mortal sin, and all the little venial sins. But she does not confess that third mortal sin.

Did the woman have a good confession? O dear, no. Our Lord has made confession so easy for us, and He asks only that we confess all our mortal sins, be sorry for them, and be willing to try hard to avoid them in the future. This is not much. No, not when we consider what Jesus had to do to pay for our sins.

BEFORE CONFESSION

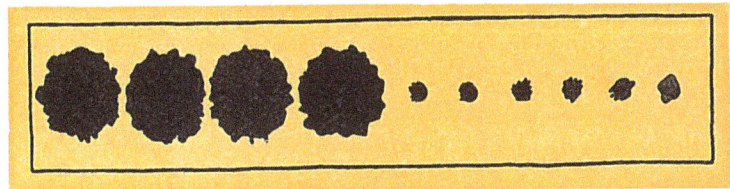

AFTER CONFESSION

If we do not do all of these things—especially if we hide one of our mortal sins—then *we do not make a good confession.* That means that *none* of the woman's sins was forgiven. What is worse, she has committed a grave sin by hiding that third mortal sin in her confession. So when the woman leaves the confessional, her soul is even dirtier and uglier than when she entered it. Now she has four mortal sins and six venial sins.

This was not a good choice, was it? It is good to be ashamed of our sins. But we know that Jesus forgave *all* sins, even very bad ones. He loves us and wants us to be in heaven with Him forever. So he said to his Apostles: "Whose sins you shall forgive, they are forgiven them." He made them priests and gave them the power to forgive sins. We must trust Our Lord and trust His priests to hear all of our sins, even the really bad ones. For who wants to go to confession, only to gain more sin? That is silly.

But there is still hope for that woman. If she comes back to confession again, this time she must confess all her mortal sins—not leaving any out. And she must also confess the sin of hiding her mortal sin during her previous confession. God will forgive her, and then her soul will be clean again.

3. The third person waiting in line is a boy. He has two mortal sins on his soul, and seven venial sins. But when he examines his conscience, he does not find the second mortal sin. He has forgotten it.

He wants to confess well, so he tells the priest the one mortal sin he remembers, and then all the venial sins.

Did the boy have a good confession? Yes, he did. Why? He did not omit that second mortal sin on purpose, he had honestly forgotten about it. If he had remembered it, he would have confessed it.

What happens with that second mortal sin then? Our Lord sees into the boy's heart, and He knows that the boy had the intention of confessing well. He knows that he is not hiding the sin on purpose.

So God absolves him of all his sins—yes, even that second mortal sin. And the boy comes out of the confessional happy, with his nice clean soul.

If he later remembers that sin he has forgotten, then he must confess it the next time he goes to confession, for he knows that all mortal sins must be confessed… unless they are honestly forgotten. Then, as long as we do our best to confess well, they are forgiven too. What a good God we have!

BEFORE CONFESSION

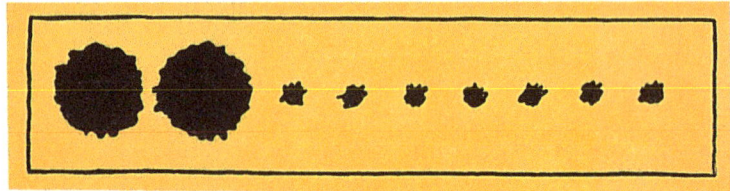

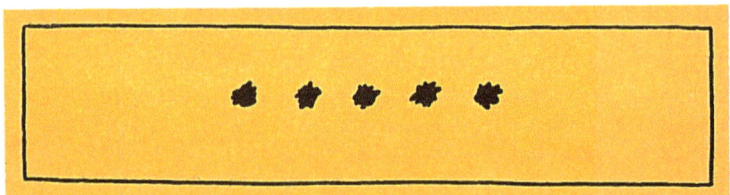

AFTER CONFESSION

4. The fourth in line for confession is a girl. She has examined her conscience, and has found just five venial sins, no mortal sins. What should she confess?

Our Lord has commanded only that all mortal sins should be confessed, but those who want to keep their souls clean from spots know it is wise to confess even the venial sins. Confessing them will give her extra grace to avoid sin in future too. So she will confess all her venial sins. And when she leaves the confessional, all of the spots will be cleaned off her soul and she will be clean and pure and fit for heaven.

BEFORE CONFESSION

AFTER CONFESSION

Some children are afraid to confess their sins to the priest. But this is silly. Priests have to go to confession too. They know that sometimes it is hard to be good. And they have heard all sorts of things in the confessional before. Do not think that your sins are too terrible or embarrassing, but tell them bravely and honestly so that you will not be like the woman who made her soul uglier with a bad confession.

The priest will never tell your sins to anyone. Even if your mother were to ask the priest, "Did my son (or daughter) commit this sin?" he will never tell her. For God has set a very grave seal on the things that are told in confession. If a priest reveals these things, he endangers his immortal soul. No priest would ever wish to do this.

There is a story of a priest, St. John Nepomucene, who lived in Prague many years ago. He was the confessor of the Queen. But the King was a jealous and suspicious man, and he wanted to know what the Queen had confessed. He demanded that the priest reveal this to him. Of course, he refused. This made the king very angry, and he threw John in prison. Still he refused to reveal what the Queen had told him in confession. Next the king had John tortured with fire, but he remained steadfast. Finally the king threatened him, "If you do not tell me, I will kill you." But the priest would rather die than endanger his soul by revealing what the queen had confessed.

So the king had John Nepomucene bound hand and foot and cast into the river, where he drowned. But God made this deed known by casting beautiful lights like stars upon the water where John lay. His body was then buried with great reverence.

Many years later, when his tomb was opened, the saint's body had crumbled into dust—all except his tongue, which was fresh and alive just like ours. In this way God showed great honor to this priest who chose death rather than to displease God.

AFTER A BAD CONFESSION: A CHILD OF THE DEVIL

AFTER A GOOD CONFESSION: A CHILD OF GOD

REITH. '27.

We know not the day, nor the hour, when death will come for us. How happy is the child who has made regular confession a habit in order to keep his white robe of grace clean. He has received Communion often, to strengthen his soul. When the time comes, he is ready to be brought by his Good Angel before God, who will say to him, "Well done, good and faithful servant! Enter into the joy of your Lord." And there will be great rejoicing in heaven on that day. And he will be happy forever in heaven, with all the angels and saints.

EDITOR'S NOTE:

This book began its life as *Het Prentenboek van de Kinderbiecht*, a book written in the 1920s by Brother Maria Cassianus Versteeg (1884-1956). He was a member of a religious community in the Netherlands which operated schools in Den Bosch and Tilburg, as well as a boys orphanage. In order to help support themselves, as well as to create opportunities for the orphaned boys to learn a useful trade, the Brothers set up a printing house in Tilburg. This highly successful and influential press, called the *Drukkerij van het RK Jongensweeshuis,* printed more than 11,000 titles over the course of its existence between 1846 and 1959. Most were children's books, both recreational and educational, some of which have since become sought-after collectibles. Many of these books were imaginatively illustrated by Bernard Reith, whose prolific work began with comic books and included regular contributions to the Dutch Catholic weekly magazine, *Catholic Illustration.*

We discovered this book and its companion *Het Prentenboek van de Eerste H. Communie* (My Picture Book of First Communion) thanks to its marvelous illustrations. However, in the process of translating it from the original Dutch, we found the text to be less than ideal. (We wondered whether perhaps it was written with the intention of scaring the orphanage boys into behaving?) Nevertheless, the illustrations alone were so compelling that we chose to persevere...even if that meant completely rewriting the text to accompany them.

Of course, it would be rather incongruous to have illustrations like these alongside a modern 21st-century text. So we relied heavily on the work of Mother Mary Loyola, our favorite author, who would have been alive at the time these books were originally published. It is for this reason that I do not claim authorship of these two books; using a basic outline derived from a rough translation of the original Dutch, I borrowed heavily from Mother Loyola, so I prefer to say only that I *adapted* and *edited* this book, based on the original by M.C. Versteeg.

In Christ,
Lisa Bergman
St. Augustine Academy Press
Feast of the Nativity of the B.V.M.

©2020 by St. Augustine Academy Press
ISBN: 978-1-64051-082-1

Nihil Obstat:
Reverend Scott McCawley
Censor Deputatus
September 1, 2020

Imprimatur:
Most Reverend Richard E. Pates
Apostolic Administrator
Diocese of Joliet
September 1, 2020